T0047556

Men-at-Arms • 287

Byzantine Armies

AD 1118–1461

Ian Heath • Illustrated by Angus McBride

Series editor Martin Windrow

First published in Great Britain in 1995 by Osprey Publishing,
Midland House, West Way, Botley, Oxford OX2 0PH, UK
44-02 23rd St, Suite 219, Long Island City, NY 11101, USA
Email: info@ospreypublishing.com

Osprey Publishing is part of the Osprey Group.

© 1995 Osprey Publishing Ltd.

All rights reserved. Apart from any fair dealing for the purpose of private study, research,
criticism or review, as permitted under the Copyright, Designs and Patents Act, 1988,
no part of this publication may be reproduced, stored in a retrieval system, or transmitted
in any form or by any means, electronic, electrical, chemical, mechanical, optical,
photocopying, recording or otherwise, without the prior written permission of the
copyright owner. Enquiries should be addressed to the Publishers.

Transferred to digital print on demand 2012

First published 1995
15th impression 2011

Printed and bound by Cadmus Communications, USA

A CIP catalogue record for this book is available from the British Library.

ISBN: 978 1 85532 347 6

Series Editor: Martin Windrow
Filmset in Great Britain by Keyspools Ltd.

Artist's note

Readers may care to note that the original paintings from which the colour plates in this book
were prepared are available for private sale. All reproduction copyright whatsoever is retained
by the Publisher. All enquiries should be addressed to:

Scorpio
158 Mill Road
HAILSHAM
East Sussex
BN27 2SH

scorpiopaintings@btinternet.com

The Publishers regret that they can enter into no correspondence upon this matter.

The Woodland Trust

Osprey Publishing is supporting the Woodland Trust, the UK's leading woodland
conservation charity, by funding the dedication of trees.

www.ospreypublishing.com

BYZANTINE ARMIES AD 1118–1461

INTRODUCTION

The Byzantine Empire's disastrous defeat by the Seljuk Turks at Manzikert in 1071 effectively marked the end of what is often described as the 'middle' period of Byzantine history. Thereafter, surrounded on all sides by younger, more vigorous nations, and with its own financial and manpower resources progressively dwindling, the once all-powerful Empire slipped into a steady decline which – though encountering occasional, sometimes lengthy, periods of remission – was to gradually gather speed and, ultimately, to prove terminal. However, the Empire's demise was anything but peaceful, and, one way or another, for much of the last four centuries of its existence it was to find itself in a state of virtually constant war.

Seljuk horsemen of the 12th century in light armour comprising helmet and lamellar corselet. Note that the lance is wielded two-handed. Though the majority of Seljuks in Byzantine service were horse-archers some are known to have been armoured.

MILITARY CHRONOLOGY

1118 Death of Alexius I Komnenos.

1122 In their last inroad into Byzantine territory, the Patzinaks are defeated at the Battle of Eski Zagra. The Cumans subsequently occupy their lands.

1124–26 War with Venice.

1128 Hungarians invade the Empire as far south as Philippopolis (Plovdiv) before being driven back.

1136–39 John II Komnenos (1118–43) having, despite numerous reverses, recovered a sizeable portion of Anatolia from the Turks during the previous two decades, reconquers Cilician Armenia and campaigns in Northern Syria, receiving the allegiance of the Crusader principality of Antioch after besieging the city (1137–38).

1146 Major Byzantine expedition against the

Seljuk Turks, though successful, achieves little.

1147 Second Crusade passes through Constantinople.

1147–48 Roger II of Sicily attacks Euboea, Thebes and Corinth, and occupies Corfu until he is expelled.

1149–52 Manuel I Komnenos (1143–80) crushes Serb rebellion and defeats the Hungarian army which comes to its aid (1150) before attacking Hungary itself. Renewed conflict in 1155–56 again ends in Hungarian defeat.

1152 Punitive expedition against Cilician Armenia.

1155–58 Attempting to recover the Empire's lost Italian possessions, Byzantines are victorious over Sicilian Normans at the Battle of Andria (1155). Despite this and other successes, however, the expedition eventually fails. Last Byzantine troops withdrawn from Italy in 1158.

1158–61 A series of expeditions against the Seljuk Turks results in a treaty favourable to the Empire.

1161–64 Combined forces of Byzantines from Cilicia and Latins from Jerusalem and Antioch active in Syria until defeated by Nur ed-Din of Aleppo at Battle of Artah.

1165–67 War resumes between Hungary and the Empire. Byzantine victory over the Hungarians at Battle of Semlin (1167) results in recovery of Dalmatia, Croatia, Bosnia and Sirmium.

1169 Failure of a joint Byzantine-Latin expedition against Damietta.

1171–77 War with Venice following Manuel I's arrest of all Venetians within the Empire. Venetians capture Ragusa 1171 and occupy Chios 1171–72 until chased off by Byzantine fleet. Joint Venetian-Sicilian attack on Byzantine protectorate of Ancona in 1173 is also defeated. Fighting ends inconclusively in 1177, peace terms not being settled until 1183.

1172 Serbian resistance is temporarily crushed.

1176 In a campaign intended to eliminate the Sultanate of Rum, Manuel I is disastrously defeated by the Seljuks at the Battle of Myriokephalon. Considerable tracts of Anatolia once again slip from Imperial control in consequence, despite several Byzantine successes between 1176–80.

1181–83 A spate of rebellions follows the death of Manuel I.

1184 Cyprus secedes from the Empire under its governor and self-styled Emperor, Isaac Komnenos.

1185 Sicilian Normans sack Durazzo (Dyrrachion) and Thessalonika, the Empire's

The Byzantine Empire c. 1180.

Right: Frontiers of the Nicaean and Latin Empires c. 1214, and of the Byzantine Empire c. 1265

second-largest city, but are eventually defeated. Sicilians also assist Isaac of Cyprus to defeat a Byzantine expedition sent to recover the island.

1186 Bulgaria and Serbia secede from the Empire.

1191 King Richard I of England conquers Cyprus and sells it to the Templars.

1202 Alexius IV, son of deposed Emperor Isaac II Angelos (1185–95), persuades Venetians and Latins mustering for the Fourth Crusade to assist him in recovering throne from usurper Alexius III (1195–1203).

1203 Venetians and Crusaders take Constantinople. Isaac II restored, with Alexius IV as co-Emperor.

1204 Isaac and Alexius are dethroned and replaced by Alexius V Doukas, who flees when Venetians and Crusaders retake Constantinople in April and establish their own 'Latin Empire'. Principal territories remaining under Byzantine rule are the Empire of Nicaea, the Despotate of Epiros, and the Empire of Trebizond. Despite victories at the Battles of Poimanenon and Adramyttion, an immediate Latin attempt to overwhelm the Nicaean Byzantines fails.

1205 Defeat of the Latins by the Bulgarians at the Battle of Adrianople obliges them to recall their forces from Asia Minor, relieving pressure on the Nicaeans.

1211 Battle of Antioch-in-Pisidia. Alliance of Latins, Seljuks and Trapezuntine Byzantines is defeated by Theodore I Laskaris of Nicaea (1204–22). The deposed Emperor Alexius III is captured fighting alongside the Seljuks.

1212 Theodore Laskaris defeats David Komnenos, independent ruler of Byzantine Paphlagonia since 1204, and overruns most of his lands.

1214 Nicaeans overrun western portion of Empire of Trebizond, David of Paphlagonia defeated and killed by Seljuks.

1215 Epirote Byzantines conquer much of Macedonia.

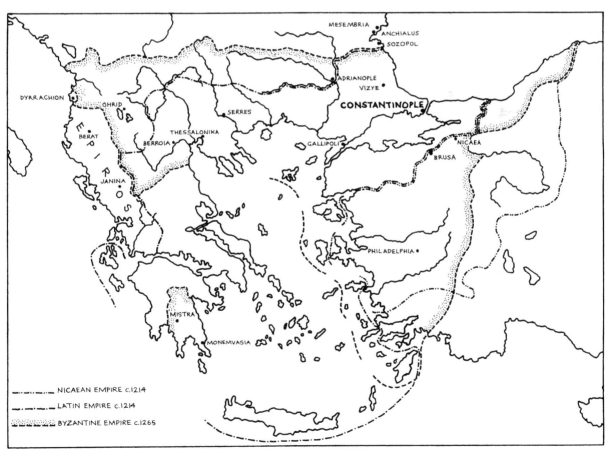

----------- NICAEAN EMPIRE c.1214
—·—·— LATIN EMPIRE c.1214
▒▒▒▒▒ BYZANTINE EMPIRE c.1265

1218	Theodore Doukas of Epiros (1215–30) commences a series of successful campaigns against the Latins and Bulgarians that extends over the next six years.	1235	Joint Nicaean-Bulgarian attack on Constantinople defeated by Venetians.
1224	Theodore Doukas recaptures Thessalonika, thenceforward calling himself Emperor. John III Doukas Vatatzes of Nicaea (1222–54) defeats the Latins at the second Battle of Poimanenon.	1238	John III provides a contingent of Byzantine troops to fight for the German emperor Frederick II in Italy.

1218 — Theodore Doukas of Epiros (1215–30) commences a series of successful campaigns against the Latins and Bulgarians that extends over the next six years.

1224 — Theodore Doukas recaptures Thessalonika, thenceforward calling himself Emperor. John III Doukas Vatatzes of Nicaea (1222–54) defeats the Latins at the second Battle of Poimanenon.

1225 — John III signs a treaty with the Latin Empire obliging its forces to withdraw from most of Asia Minor, and in addition conquers much of Thrace.

1230 — Battle of Klokotnitza. Theodore Doukas of Thessalonika defeated by Bulgarians, who overrun Macedonia and Thrace. His 'Empire' fragments into three smaller autonomous units, Thessalonika, Epiros and Thessaly.

1233 — John III defeats Leo Gabalas, Despot of Rhodes.

1235 — Joint Nicaean-Bulgarian attack on Constantinople defeated by Venetians.

1238 — John III provides a contingent of Byzantine troops to fight for the German emperor Frederick II in Italy.

1243 — Following defeat of the Seljuks by the Mongols at the Battle of Kuzadagh, Sultan Ka Khosrou II signs treaty of alliance with Nicaea. Emperor Manuel of Trebizond (1238–63) becomes a Mongol vassal.

1246 — Nicaeans capture Thessalonika from Epirotes and reconquer Adrianople and much of southern Macedonia from Bulgarians.

1251–52 — Nicaean and Epirote Byzantines in conflict until a frontier, advantageous to the former, is agreed between them.

1254–56 — Bulgarians try to recover lost territory following death of John III of Nicaea but are eventually beaten.

1257–59 — Epirote campaign to recapture Thessalonika from Nicaeans culminates in Battle of Pelagonia, in which Epirotes and their Latin allies are decisively defeated.

1261 — Michael VIII Palaeologos (1261–82) usurps Nicaean throne from kinsman John IV Laskaris (1258–61). His general Alexius Strategopoulos recaptures Constantinople, marking the end of the Latin Empire.

1262 — The Prince of Achaea, captured at the Battle of Pelagonia, hands over to Michael VIII the fortresses of Mistra, Monemvasia and Maina in the Morea in exchange for his freedom, but war against the Latins, Venetians and Epirotes ensues.

1263 — Byzantines defeated by Achaeans at the Battle of Prinitza. This year also marks the final confrontation between Byzantine and Hungarian armies, when the former advance into western Bulgaria and threaten Hungarian puppet-state of Vidin. Michael VIII captures Bulgarian Black Sea ports (Mesembria, Anchialus, Sozopol and Develtus).

1264 — Battle of Makryplagi. Byzantines defeated by Achaean Franks.

Emperor Manuel I Komnenos and his consort Maria, daughter of Raymond, Prince of Antioch. (ENI Collection)

Shield graffiti of the 12th–13th century from the Bucoleon Palace in Constantinople. The non-heraldic patterns certainly seem Eastern rather than Western, but there is no way of knowing whether they represent the shields of Byzantine soldiers, Latin mercenaries or Western crusaders.

1273 Epirotes under John I Doukas of Thessaly (1271–89), supported by Latins, rout Byzantine forces besieging Neopatras. These withdraw to the coast, just in time to reinforce their fleet and defeat a Veneto-Latin squadron at Battle of Demetrias.

1277 Epirotes defeat Byzantines at the Battle of Pharsala.

1280–82 War between the Empire and Charles of Anjou's 'kingdom of Albania'. The Angevins are defeated at Berat 1281, and a year later rebellion in Sicily prevents Charles from pursuing the conflict further.

1281–85 War between the Empire and Venice.

1282 Serbs begin conquest of Byzantine Macedonia, taking Skoplje.

1292–93 Byzantines campaign against Despotate of Epiros.

1296 Durazzo, having changed hands several times, is finally lost (to Serbs). By coming to the aid of its Genoese allies the Empire becomes involved in a war between Genoa and Venice, the resultant conflict dragging on until 1302.

1302 The Ottoman Turks win their first victory over the Byzantines at Bapheus. Roger de Flor's mercenary 'Catalan Grand Company' is hired by Andronikos II (1282–1328). It arrives at Constantinople in 1303 and de Flor is created *megas doux*.

1304 The Catalan Grand Company scores victories over the Turks at Philadelphia, Tyre, Ani and the Iron Gates. Bulgarians attack Byzantine frontier. Andronikos II cedes Chios to a Genoese adventurer.

1305 Following the Byzantine-instigated murder of Roger de Flor, the Catalan Grand Company defeats the Byzantines at the Battle of Apros and goes on the rampage through Thrace. Bulgarians take advantage of Byzantine discomfiture to recover Black Sea ports of Mesembria, Anchialus and Sozopol.

1307 Death of Alauddin III, Sultan of Rum. Seljuk sultanate disintegrates.

1308 Rhodes conquered by the Knights Hospitaller.

1309–11 Catalan Grand Company overruns Thessaly, culminating in a decisive victory over Latins at Kephissos.

Emperor John VI Kantakouzenos presiding over an ecumenical council in 1351. Immediately behind the throne are eight Varangian Guards in gold-trimmed, boat-shaped white hats and blue gowns. In his Historiae Kantakouzenos mentions the 'Varangians with their axes' several times. Varangians in action at Eski Zagra in 1122 are recorded as 'armed with long shields and single-edged axes'.

Stefan Dushan, self-styled Tsar of the Greek lands of Romania 1345–55, with wife Helena (sister of his ally Tsar Ivan Alexander) and son Stefan Urosh V.

1318 Last Byzantine rulers of Epiros and Thessaly die, and are succeeded by foreign dynasties.

1321–28 Civil wars between Andronikos II and his grandson Andronikos III (1328–41) take place 1321–22 and 1327–28, culminating in the abdication of the former.

1326 Bursa falls to the Ottoman Turks, becoming their first capital.

1328 Bulgarians invade northern Thrace but are forced to withdraw.

1329 Ottoman Turks defeat the Byzantines at the Battle of Pelekanon and again, the following day, at Philokrene. Excepting Philadelphia and a few coastal towns, all of Byzantine Anatolia falls within the next few years. In the autumn Byzantines recover Chios, most of its Italian defenders subsequently taking service with the Empire.

1330 Serbian victory over the Bulgarians at Battle of Velbuzdh. Byzantines occupy various frontier towns and forts until they are defeated by Bulgarians two years later at Battle of Russocastro.

1331 Ottomans capture Nicaea.

1333–40 Andronikos III campaigns against Epirotes and Albanians, finally conquering both Epiros and Thessaly.

1334 Serbs under Stefan Dushan invade Macedonia.

1337 Ottomans capture Nikomedia.

1338 Ottomans capture Skutari.

1341–47 Civil war between Empress Anna, on behalf of her son John V Palaeologos (1341–76 and 1379–91), and John VI Kantakouzenos, ending with recognition of John VI as co-Emperor (1347–54). Stefan Dushan takes the opportunity to overrun Empire's last outposts in Albania (1343–45).

1346 Having conquered Albania and Macedonia, Stefan Dushan proclaims himself 'Emperor of the Serbs and Greeks'.

1348 Serbs conquer northern Greece, Epiros and Thessaly.

1352–57 John VI's attempt to get his son Matthew recognised as heir to the throne results in renewed civil war, John V being backed by Venice, Serbia and Bulgaria, while Genoa and the Ottoman Turks support the Kantakouzenoi. Matthew proclaimed Emperor 1353 but renounces claims 1357 in favour of John V, John VI having abdicated 1354.

1354 Ottoman capture of Gallipoli marks commencement of their conquest of the Balkans. Within a decade the Empire is reduced to a few dislocated territories comprising Constantinople, Thessalonika, the Morea, and a handful of islands and scattered cities.

1355 Serbian kingdom disintegrates following death of Stefan Dushan.

1361 Ottomans capture Didymoteichos and, following the defeat of Byzantine-Bulgarian forces at Eski Baba, Adrianople, which in 1366 becomes new Ottoman capital.

1364 Byzantines capture Anchialus.

1365 The Empire remains aloof from a coalition of Serbian, Hungarian, Bosnian and Wallachian forces which, marching to retake Adrianople, is decisively beaten by the Ottomans.

The Byzantine Empire c. 1350 (left) and c. 1403 (right).

1366 The crusader Amadeo VI of Savoy recovers Gallipoli and Mesembria for the Empire.

1371 Ottoman conquest of Serbia begins with victory over King Vukashin at the Battle of Cernomen.

1372 Bulgaria and the Empire become Ottoman vassal states.

1373–85 Civil war again racks the Empire, Andronikos IV Palaeologos (1376–79) rebelling against his father John V. Andronikos is supported by the Genoese, John by the Venetians, and both at various times by the Ottomans. John disinherits Andronikos in favour of his younger son Manuel.

1376 Andronikos IV surrenders Gallipoli to the Ottomans in exchange for their help against John V, and with Genoese assistance seizes Constantinople, capturing John and Manuel.

1379 With Venetian help, John V and Manuel escape. John agrees to supply Ottomans with troops each spring in exchange for their help in recovering Constantinople, which is agreed only on condition that Andronikos IV is nevertheless reinstated as heir. Manuel withdraws to Thessalonika.

1385 On death of Andronikos IV his son John VII is appointed ruler in Selymbria.

1387 Ottomans capture Thessalonika after a three-year siege.

1389 Decisive Ottoman victory over Serbs at the Battle of Kossovo.

1390 With Ottoman assistance John VII enters Constantinople, besieging John V in fortress of the Golden Gate until Manuel comes to his rescue. John VII then retires to Selymbria as an Ottoman vassal. In the autumn both he and Manuel are obliged to lead Byzantine contingents to assist Ottomans in capture of Philadelphia, the last Byzantine city in Asia Minor.

1392–94 Ottomans subjugate Bulgaria (1393) and Thessaly.

1394–1402 Ottoman blockade and intermittent siege of Constantinople.

1395 Ottomans defeat Byzantines in the Morea.

A 12th century depiction of a military saint. Manuscripts and murals depict Byzantine soldiers in apparently dated equipment throughout this period, so are not generally considered accurate. The consensus appears to be that though their portrayal of helmets, swords and shields is reliable, the armour is deliberately archaic. Such selective traditionalism, however, is improbable, and what seems more likely is that – barring exceptions obvious to even an untrained eye – many contemporary pictures are more accurate than is often supposed.

1396 Joint Burgundian-Hungarian expedition against the Ottomans is destroyed at Nikopolis.

1402 Ottoman siege of Constantinople is finally raised following their decisive defeat by Tamerlane at the Battle of Ankara. Momentarily weakened thereby, in 1403 the Ottomans sign a treaty with Manuel II Palaeologos (1391–1425) by which Thessalonika and numerous other towns, islands and fortresses are returned to the Empire, and all Byzantine captives are released.

1411 Having supported the wrong contender in an Ottoman civil war, Constantinople is briefly besieged.

1422 Ottomans again unsuccessfully besiege Constantinople.

1423 Thessalonika, under siege by the Ottomans, is handed over to Venice.

1427 The Morea is reorganised into three despotates based at Mistra, Glarentza and Kalavryta.

1429–30 The despots of the Morea defeat Centurione Zaccaria, Prince of Achaea, and absorb the principality following Zaccaria's death.

1430 Ottomans retake Thessalonika after an eight-year siege.

1442 Demetrios, brother of Emperor John VIII Palaeologos (1425–48), unsuccessfully besieges Constantinople supported by Ottoman troops.

1444 Moreote Byzantines capture Athens, Thebes and Boeotia.

1453 Ottomans capture Constantinople, ending the Byzantine Empire. Constantine XI Palaeologos (1448–53), the last Emperor, is killed in street-fighting after the Turks force their way into city.

1458–60 Ottomans conquer the Despotate of the Morea.

1461 Ottomans besiege and capture Trebizond.

THE BYZANTINE ARMED FORCES 1118–1453

The late Byzantine army was made up of four principal elements – a small central army based in Constantinople; various provincial armies; foreign mercenaries; and auxiliaries provided by allies and client states. Even with all these resources, however, individual 12th–14th century Byzantine field armies – with the obvious exception of those mustered for major campaigns – were invariably small, usually comprising no more than 2,000 men, but sometimes reaching 3–6,000 or, on rare occasions, 10–12,000. However, it is possible that at least some of the smaller figures derived from old records refer only to those cavalry present, and need to be multiplied several times to allow for foot-soldiers. It should also be borne in mind that even during the Empire's heyday in the 10th century Emperor Nikephoros II had considered a force of 5–6,000 cavalry as sufficient for any campaign.

The central army – called the *Tagmata* or, more usually, the *Taxeis* or *Vasilikon Allagia*, provided the nucleus of every field army until the early 13th century. It consisted predominantly of foreign mercenaries and included the Emperor's few guard units. The provincial armies were generally very small at the beginning of the period, when they probably consisted of no more than the few garrison troops permanently based in local fortresses, but they steadily increased in size in the course of the 12th century. They generally contributed contingents to the central army on campaign, but the distances that had to be covered often resulted in a considerable delay occurring before a worthwhile field army could be assembled.

In Manuel I's reign, in the second half of the 12th century, the custom began of billeting the central army throughout the provinces each winter in order to ease the strain on the Imperial treasury, and the distinction between central and provincial armies became somewhat blurred. Consequently many provincial units found themselves drafted into the central army, particularly under Theodore II (1254–58). Believing that the army's weakness resulted from its heavy dependence on foreign mercenaries, he concentrated the best of the remaining native troops in Constantinople and reduced the pay and privileges of its foreign mercenaries, declaring his intention *c*. 1255 'to build an army not of Turks, Italians or Serbs, but of Greeks'.

Not surprisingly his successor Michael VIII, having previously been commander of the army's Latin mercenaries, reverted to the employment of large numbers of foreign troops, a move which, along with his vigorous campaigns to restore the unity of the Empire, financially exhausted its resources.

When Andronikos II succeeded in 1282 he was, therefore, obliged to instigate savage cutbacks in military expenditure. In fact he was not even able to maintain the capital's central army, instead billeting it permanently on provincial householders who were obliged to feed and lodge the soldiers and their horses, allowances for this being fixed by a commission but paid only at erratic intervals. The historian Gregoras reports that the native element of the army now became 'the laughing stock of the world', with but one aim in battle – to run away as quickly as possible.

Andronikos II's plan of *c*. 1320 to introduce new taxes to finance just 1,000 men to be based in Bithynia and 2,000 more in Thrace and Macedonia was frustrated by the outbreak of the first of a series of civil wars that racked the Empire from 1321–57. The *megas domestikos* John Kantakouzenos (later Emperor John VI) instigated some reforms during the 1330s, managing for a while to enforce the obligatory service of *pronoia*-holders (see below), strengthening the frontier garrisons, and insisting that the treasury paid soldiers on time whilst on active duty, but most

A 12th century Byzantine soldier wearing a lamellar corselet, from a steatite now in Plovdiv archaeological museum, Bulgaria.

of his efforts were rendered redundant when the civil wars resumed in 1341.

Fought on both sides almost entirely by auxiliary troops provided by the Empire's common enemies, the Serbs and Ottoman Turks, these civil wars crippled Byzantine military potential beyond recovery. The Empire was left with insufficient resources to maintain more than a handful of troops. John Kantakouzenos' own army, with which he was able to capture Constantinople in 1347, comprised just 1,000 men. The Empire was left with no option but to sign a treaty acknowledging Ottoman suzerainty in 1372, and Byzantine troops were thereafter provided to fight alongside the Ottomans, starting in 1373. In 1379 John V even agreed with Sultan Murad (in return for his aid in yet another civil war) to supply him with 12,000 soldiers every spring, but the idea that the Empire could raise this many men by the late 14th century is pure fantasy. In reality its regular army had withered away to virtually nothing by this time, Sultan Bayezid's demand in 1390 that the

Empire provide him with just 100 soldiers (when Serbia was expected to provide 1,000) ably demonstrating its numerical insignificance.

Pronoiai

Many Byzantine soldiers of the post-Manzikert era were maintained by grants of land called *pronoia* ('providences' or 'solicitudes'). These were not actually a right to the land itself but rather to the revenue and labour services which the district and its inhabitants otherwise owed to the state. Though it was largely by means of such *pronoiai* that the Komneno Emperors, and especially Manuel I, re-established the central army in the 12th century, they nevertheless remained relatively uncommon until the late 13th century, and by then were already in decline.

The *pronoia*-holder, typically a native heavy cavalryman (though as early as Manuel I's reign *pronoia* were being granted to 'half-barbarians' and foreigners), was properly called a pronoiar (*pronoiarios*), but after the 13th century was more commonly known simply as a *stratiotes* or 'soldier'. Though his *pronoia* was usually in the provinces, the pronoiar himself was generally a soldier of the central army, and thus in effect an absentee landlord. He was not, however, a full-time soldier but a reservist, called out for temporary service when required but otherwise paying a tax on his revenues which helped finance field armies elsewhere. Being in many cases magnates (*dynatoi*), some pronoiars were accompanied in action by retinues made up of their *oikeioi* (kinsmen and companions) and *oiketai* (retainers), the latter sometimes including household mercenaries. The largest such retinues are unlikely to have exceeded 30–80 men, the majority probably comprising a mere handful.

Some *pronoiai*, however, of a type which were more usually referred to as *oikonomia*, were of considerably lower value, generating only a sixth to an eighth of what might be considered average revenue. These smallholdings, held by soldier-farmers, probably provided light cavalry and infantry rather than heavy cavalry, and, along with 'collective' *pronoiai*, held by two or more men together, by the mid 13th century were the principal means of maintaining

St Michael, from a 12th century Thessalonikan steatite. He appears to wear a quilted corselet.

native provincial troops, including some (or perhaps most) garrisons. Such smallholding soldiers continued to be found under Andronikos II and even later (the last effort to strengthen their numbers dates to 1372) but during the 14th century their importance rapidly declined as frontier lands were progressively abandoned to the Turks.

Initially non-hereditary, the conversion of some *pronoiai* into hereditary holdings during Michael VIII's reign was probably an attempt to stem this decline, while a sudden dramatic increase in the number of hereditary *pronoiai* in the 1340s was probably an attempt to win the support of the *dynatoi* during the civil wars. Such alienations to the provincial magnates, however, along with continuous territorial losses and the exemptions from military service which were, incomprehensibly, granted to many pronoiars, inevitably resulted in the total collapse of the *pronoia* system long before the end of the 14th century.

Unit organisation

Army sub-divisions were called by a variety of names. Units called by the middle Byzantine terms *bandon* (or *tagma*) and *moira*, originally bodies of 300 and about 1,000 men, still occasionally occur in the early part of the period, but that most commonly encountered by the 13th century was the cavalry *allagion*, commanded by an *allagator*. Though sometimes used simply as a generic term to describe a body of soldiers, the *allagion* proper, originally (in the 10th century) a 50-strong troop, had by now actually replaced the earlier *bandon*, and itself become a unit of most commonly 300, or sometimes up to 500 men. Units and multiples of 300, or nearly 300, occur repeatedly in late Byzantine sources.

In all probability *allagia* were in theory subdivided into the units of 100, 50 and 10 men that are also occasionally encountered. In battle *allagia* were grouped, usually in threes, into larger bodies called *taxeis*, *syntaxeis*, *lochoi* or sometimes *tagmata*. Confusingly, however, the last term was also still used in literary sources to describe much smaller units.

Allagia disappear with the loss of Asia Minor, and in the Empire's European possessions *megala allagia* (or 'great' *allagia*) appear in their place. Each province seems to have constituted one *megala allagia*, which was named after it (e.g., the *Thessalonikaion* from Thessalonika, the *Vizyeteikon* from Vizye, and the *Serriotikon* from Serres), and probably virtually every native soldier to be found within the province, horse and foot, garrison and reserve troops alike, was incorporated within it, whence these men were collectively referred to as *megaloallagitai*. *Megala allagia* occur from the 1280s and survived until the mid 14th century, disappearing between 1345–87 as the provinces on which they were based fell to the Turks and Serbs. Byzantine unit organisation thereafter seems to have been on an entirely ad hoc basis.

Guard units

Guard regiments that survived into the Komnenoi era at the end of the 11th century comprised the *Hetaireia*, the *Exkoubitoi*, the *Athanatoi* and the *Varrangoi* or Varangian Guard, to which Alexius I had added the *Vestiaritai*, responsible for guarding the Imperial treasuries. Of these units, only the Varangians survived Alexius' death, to which the *Vardariotai*, actually a police rather than a guard

A 13th century Byzantine helmet. Brimmed helmets (with the 'brim' sometimes little more than a flared rim) were the predominant Byzantine type in the 12th–13th centuries, but during the 14th century they seem to have been displaced by bascinets similar to those of Western Europe.

Military saint from a 13th century icon, with characteristic Byzantine long triangular shield. The face of the shield appears to be decorated with small crosses, while the inner surface is painted with vertical blue and white stripes and red spots.

Paramonai. According to Pseudo-Kodinos the full strength of the entire *Taxeis* or central army after 1261 was 6,000 men, organised in 12 *allagia*, so none of the guard regiments it included can have been very large. The guard that Kantakouzenos established to protect Emperor John V in 1341 consisted of just 500 men plus 'as many axe-bearing barbarians [i.e. Varangians] as were then in service'.

The existence of the Varangian Guard is still recorded in 1404, and it is not impossible that the unit survived until the very end of the Empire. However, it has also been suggested that in the 15th century its duties may have passed to a Cretan guard unit, the existence of which is recorded in 1422. It is possible, even likely, that during the siege of Constantinople in 1453 this unit was represented by the Cretans who defended three towers near the Blachernae Palace so tenaciously that the Turks allowed them to depart unmolested. Certainly 'palace troops' are mentioned during the final siege. Another foreign guard regiment which, it has been suggested, survived at least as late as 1437, consisted of Catalans, John VI Kantakouzenos having established a 500-strong unit from these in the mid 14th century.

One final bodyguard unit comprised the Emperor's own *oikeioi* and *oiketai*, who are invariably to be found accompanying him in action. Kinnamos, for instance, records Manuel I being accompanied in 1146 by a regiment 'consisting of those nearest him in blood, among whom were many of his most intimate associates and those who had married his sisters', while Nicolò Barbaro tells us that Constantine XI, when defending Constantinople in 1453, had an escort consisting of 'a great part of his barons and knights'.

Provincial armies and frontier defence

The provinces or *themata*, the administrative divisions into which the Empire had been divided in the middle Byzantine period, were gradually re-structured during the century following the Battle of Manzikert, so that by the 1150s they basically comprised: in Anatolia – Cappadocia, Chaldia, Cilicia, Kibyrraioton, Mylasa Melanoudion, Neokastra, Nikomedia, Opsikion, Optimaton, Paphlagonia-Boukellarion, and Thrakesion; and in Europe – Berroia, Branicevo-Nish, Dyrrachion-Ohrid, Hellas, Macedonia, Nikopolis, Paristrion, Peloponnese, Serbia, Skoplje, Strymon, Thessalonika, Thrace, and

unit, was added by either John II or, more probably, Manuel I. Despite occurring in Pseudo-Kodinos' *Book of Offices* of *c.* 1355 the Vardariots seem to have disappeared after 1272, apparently being replaced by the *Paramonai*, a native regiment consisting of one *allagion* of infantry and one of cavalry. Outside Pseudo-Kodinos this unit is last mentioned in 1315. Two other 13th century units still mentioned in the *Book of Offices*, the *Mourtatoi* (infantry archers of mixed Greco-Turkish parentage) and the *Tzakones* (a mace-armed bodyguard of marines), appear to have constituted guard regiments only briefly, and for most of the century the only palace units remained the Varangian Guard and the Vardariots or

Voleron. Comparison with earlier lists of *themata* will show that few of the 10th–11th century provinces had survived intact.

As Byzantine territory steadily shrank provincial and frontier defence became effectively synonymous. Each of the provinces, until the 13th century, continued to be governed by a *doux* ('duke'), who was simultaneously commander of whatever armed forces it could muster. Beneath him the military responsibility for each town was in the hands of an officer called a *kastrophylax* or 'fortress guard'. However, by the 14th century the *themata*, already much smaller than their middle period counterparts, had been replaced by an even smaller administrative unit, most often called a *katepanikon*, centred on a *kastron* (a walled town with a central keep). To fulfil his military duties the governor, now known as a *kephale* or 'head', was henceforth assisted by the *kastrophylax* (specifically responsible for the physical condition of the province's defences), and also by an officer called by the Turkish-derived title of *tzaousios*, who commanded the garrison. In wartime the *kephale* assumed the role of quartermaster general and administered the provision of supplies to his troops in the field, who in all probability were commanded by the *tzaousios*.

Most sizeable provincial, and all frontier, towns constituted such *kastra*. Their defences were built and maintained largely by taxes levied on local land-owners and monasteries, and wherever it could be afforded they boasted their own permanent garrisons. These, generally hired by means of some local arrangement rather than via the central administration, were usually natives rather than foreign mercenaries. It was they who constituted the nucleus of each provincial army.

However, many members of such garrisons were not technically soldiers at all, but rather civilian watchmen called *tzakones*, performing occasional or sometimes permanent guard duty (*tzakonike* or *vigla*). Such civilian watchmen similarly manned the simple watch-towers (*pyrgoi*) built in large numbers during the 13th–15th centuries, particularly in Thrace and Macedonia. Indeed, maintenance of the Empire's defences relied heavily on the efforts of the local population for both manpower and finance, though it is on record that the money sometimes levied to hire additional men was frequently given only with 'very bad grace'.

In frontier districts the local population was often reinforced by means of military colonies, some-

Cavalry engagement from the Skyllitzes Codex (second half of the 13th century). The protagonists wear hip-length scale and lamellar corselets, and helmets with neck-guards made of leather strips. (ENI Collection)

times consisting of foreign ethnic groups (either mercenaries or prisoners-of-war) but usually of natives, encouraged by a variety of inducements, such as tax exemption, and the granting of *pronoiai* to 'the more illustrious', not just to settle in such insecure areas, but to participate actively in their defence. During the second half of the 13th century numerous such militiamen found themselves forcibly converted into part-time soldiers, subsequently holding their lands in exchange for paid, but obligatory, military service. Demoralised by these reforms many fled or, when mustered, dispersed to protect their own property. Some even defected to the Turks. This led to the gradual disintegration of the Anatolian frontier, a process accelerated by Michael VIII's preoccupation with the Empire's western defences. By the end of the 13th century the Anatolian provinces had largely been lost and their armies had all but disintegrated. Some troops were still sent to Europe from Anatolia as late as 1328, but thereafter they ceased to exist.

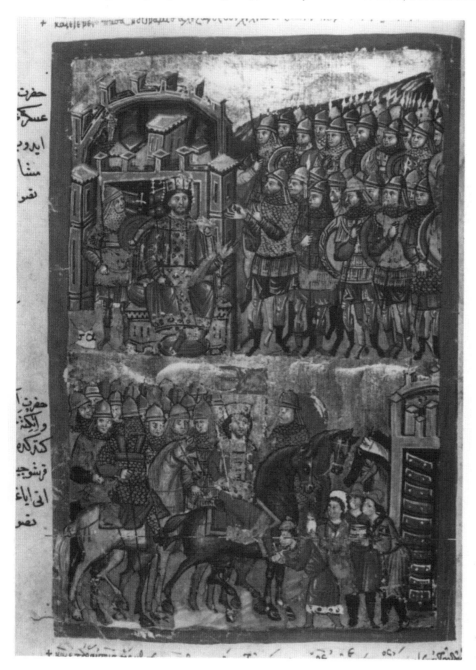

Left: (Top) Mid 14th century Byzantine soldiers from the Romance of Alexander the Great, wearing a mixture of mail and lamellar corselets, mail hoods, and brimmed helmets with leather aventails. (Below) Also from the Romance of Alexander the Great, this portrayal of 14th century Byzantine heavy cavalry is probably one of the most accurate to be found. Note in particular the fully-armoured figure at left. Separate mail hoods, as opposed to mail aventails attached to the helmet, were in use by the late 12th century. Note the dragon-embroidered flag; the historian Choniates describes flags he saw accompanying Isaac II's army in 1187 as 'representations of dragons suspended on poles and blowing in the wind'. (Instituto Ellenico di Venezia)

The navy

The decline of Byzantine naval power which began in the 10th century had been briefly arrested by Alexius I Komnenos, but continued following his death in 1118. Thereafter successive Emperors largely depended on the Italian maritime republics of Venice, Genoa and Pisa for naval defence, these agreeing to provide ships and men in exchange for pay and favourable trading concessions within the Empire. An agreement made with Venice in 1187 is fairly typical. This set out that, at six months' notice, the republic would provide 40–100 galleys (equipped at the Empire's expense), on which three out of every four Venetian colonists within the Empire were expected to serve. In the event of an unexpected emergency the colonists were expected to serve aboard Byzantine vessels instead.

The native fleet was revived by Manuel I, so that for the expedition to Damietta in 1169 he was able to provide 12 large warships, 150 galleys and 60 transports. However, the decline resumed under his successors. By 1196 there were only 30 galleys still afloat, and when the Fourth Crusade appeared before Constantinople in 1203 the 20 worm-eaten hulks that remained were only fit to be used as fireships.

Michael VIII rebuilt the fleet again following the Nicaean recovery of Constantinople in 1261, crewing it with *Gazmouloi*, *Tzakones* and *Prosalentai*. The *Gazmouloi* were Greco-Latin half-breeds, said to 'derive zealousness in battle and prudence from the Byzantines, and impetuosity and audacity from the Latins'. The *Tzakones* and *Prosalentai*, however, were natives; the former, from the Morea, served as marines, while the latter provided oarsmen.

This reconstituted navy comprised 80 ships by 1283 when, shortly after his accession, Andronikos II disbanded it and dismissed at least the *Gazmouloi* and *Tzakones* in an attempt to reduce costs, instead depending entirely on Genoese vessels (of which 50–60 had been hired by 1291). His own plans to resurrect the fleet by the construction of 20 galleys *c.*1320 appear to have been still-born, leaving his grandson Andronikos III to initiate its final revival. He re-employed the *Gazmouloi* and, probably, the *Prosalentai* following Andronikos II's abdication in 1328 (they are still recorded at least as late as 1422 and 1361 respectively), and by 1332 was able to

Constantinople under attack, from the Manasses Codex *of 1344–45. The lower defender is armed with a crossbow, or tzangra (whence crossbowmen were called tzangratoroi). Considered a foreign weapon (it was often called 'the Latin bow') the crossbow remained a rarity in the Empire even in the 14th century, when Byzantine writers still felt obliged to describe it to their readers in considerable detail. Normally it was only used in defence of fortifications, and not in the open field, though Byzantine troops confronting Richard the Lionheart's landing on Cyprus in 1191 included crossbowmen.*

contribute 10 galleys to a naval league against the Turks. However, though the impressment of merchant vessels might occasionally boost the apparent strength of Byzantine fleets to 100 or even 200 vessels, 10 remained the maximum number of actual warships ever encountered after this date, as in 1352, 1396, 1421 and 1453.

The chain of command

Though a sophisticated hierarchy of military ranks existed in the late Byzantine period, their bestowal reflected the degree of favour with which the recipient was regarded by the Emperor rather than denoting that he could fulfil the particular military responsibilities implied by his title; and it was his hierarchical rank that qualified him for military command, not the nominal function of the post he held. It is therefore unsurprising to find that many field-commanders actually held civilian ranks, and that naval officers often commanded armies while army officers sometimes commanded fleets.

Supreme commander of the Empire's armed forces was, of course, the Emperor, who customarily led major expeditions in person. The complex, theoretical chain of command beneath him is set out in Pseudo-Kodinos' *Book of Offices* (c. 1355) as comprising: 1. Despot; 2. *Sebastokrator*; 3. Caesar; 4. *Megas domestikos* (senior army commander in the absence of the preceding); 5. *Megas doux* (commander of the navy); 6. *Protostrator* (deputy of 4); 7. *Megas stratopedarches* (prefect of the militia, intro-

This page from the Romance of Alexander the Great shows (at the top) cavalrymen on lamellar-barded horses, and unusually heavily-armoured archers. The archers have small circular shields on their left arms for protection as commended in 10th century Byzantine military manuals. (Instituto Ellenico di Venezia)

A cavalry engagement from the mid 14th century Romance of Alexander the Great, *its imagery probably prompted by the Empire's bloody civil wars of 1321–57. The combatants wear mail corselets, fabric hoods and bascinets, one or two adding mail chausses. Leather breast-bands and shoulder-harness are also in evidence. (Instituto Ellenico di Venezia)*

duced by Theodore II in the mid 13th century and responsible for the commissariat); 8. *Megas primmikerios* (commander of the Imperial retinue); 9. *Megas konostablos* (commander of the Latin mercenaries, introduced by John III Vatatzes); 10. *Megas droungarios* (commander of the Watch); 11. *Megas hetaireiarches* (nominally commander of the army's mercenary elements); 12. *Epi tou stratou* (prefect of the army, another 13th century introduction); 13. Domestic of the *Scholae* (once the senior army commander, but now a ceremonial post); 14. *Megas droungarios* of the Fleet (deputy of 5); 15. *Protospatharios* (commander of the Emperor's sword-bearers); 16. *Megas arkhon* (introduced by Theodore II as commander of his household troops, but now deputy of 8); 17. *Megas tzaousios* (sergeant-at-arms of the Imperial retinue, responsible for maintenance of order during Court ceremonies); 18. *Skouterios* (Imperial standard-bearer); 19. *Amyriales* (admiral, naval third-in-command); 20. *Megas akolouthos* (commander of the Varangian Guard); 21. *Arkhon tou Allagion* (in the early 13th century commander of the Imperial retinue but by the 14th century deputy of 16); 22. *Protallagator* (commander of the *Paramonai*); 23. Domestic of the Walls (responsible for Constantinople's defences); 24. *Vestiarios* (naval fourth-in-command); 25. *Hetaireiarches* (deputy of 11); 26. *Stratopedarches* of the *Mourtatoi*; 27. *Stratopedarches* of the *Tzakones*; 28. *Stratopedarches* of the 'cavalry-men with one horse'; 29. *Stratopedarches* of the

crossbowmen; and 30. *Protokomes* (premier count, a naval officer).

Amongst the civilian officials found in command of armies in the 13th–15th centuries were the *pinkernes* (Imperial butler), *mesazon* (court mediator), *parakoimomenos* (chamberlain) and *protovestiarites* (treasurer of the Imperial wardrobe).

Firearms and the Empire

The use of gunpowder artillery crept steadily eastwards from Europe in the course of the 14th century: its use is first recorded in Hungary in 1354, in the western Balkans in 1378, and in Serbia during the 1380s. The Ottoman Turks had cannon by *c.* 1400 at the latest. Handguns followed, being in widespread use throughout the Balkans by the 1420s. However, this late mediaeval arms race largely passed the Empire by. Despite an apparent but questionable reference to the use of guns by John VII in 1390 (against the fortress of the Golden Gate, held by John V), and though the Byzantines certainly *knew* of firearms by 1392 at the latest, it seems unlikely that they actually possessed any of their own until about 1422, in which year, according to Chalkokondyles, guns were used to defend Constantinople against the Ottomans. These were probably obtained via the Venetians and Genoese – certainly there is no evidence that the Byzantines ever manufactured any themselves. The only record of a gun-founder in Constantinople dates to as late as 1452, and when the

Mail-armoured Byzantine cavalry of the Palaeologian period from *the* Romance of Alexander the Great. *(Instituto Ellenico di Venezia)*

Emperor could not afford to hire him he sold his services to the Turks instead.

The Byzantines never used gunpowder artillery in the field, and the only place known to have been defended by guns was Constantinople itself, which had an unknown but clearly insufficient number by 1453. These included some large enough (firing 40kg/90lb shot) that according to Chalkokondyles and Leonard of Chios, both eye-witnesses, their discharge 'shook the walls, and did more damage to them than to the enemy'. Leonard adds that others 'could not be fired very often because of the shortage of powder and shot', but that when they were they caused 'great destruction of men' amongst the Turks.

Handguns may not have been adopted by the Byzantines at all, there being no evidence that they were beyond a reference by the historian Doukas (who wrote *c*. 1462) that Byzantines defending Constantinople in 1453 'shot lead balls which were propelled by powder, 5 and 10 at a time, and as small as Pontic walnuts'. However, the fact that he was not himself present at the siege, and his use of almost the same words to describe handguns used by the Hungarians in 1440, render his account suspect. Certainly

none of the eye-witness accounts of 1453 refer t Byzantine soldiers using handguns. Even so, th Byzantines had several names for the handgun, call ing it either a *molybdobolon* ('lead-thrower') or else *skopeta* or *touphax* (corruptions of the Italian an Turkish words for handguns, *schioppetto* and *tufenk*)

'SOLDIERS HIRED AMONGST ALL NATIONS'

Soldiers of the late Byzantine period mostly fell int one of three distinct categories: pronoiars; smallhold ing soldier-farmers; or foreigners, either auxiliarie or mercenaries. Distinctions between these catego ries were often blurred. Some auxiliaries receive pay, for instance, numerous mercenaries receive *pronoiai*, and some smallholding soldiers receive pay as well as land. But in broad terms pronoiar were the least common troop-type and mercenaries/ auxiliaries by far the most common. Indeed, th greater part of all late Byzantine armies consisted o foreigners, and the native element was so small tha foreign commentators often barely noticed its exist ence.

The importance of mercenaries had steadily in creased following the loss of Asia Minor and it manpower reserves in the late 11th century, despit the Empire's increasing difficulty in paying them a its economy progressively collapsed. Their employ ment was simply an acknowledgement of the fact tha well-armed 'professional' soldiers were usually more loyal, and undeniably more effective, than native troops.

Although a few were native Byzantines and oth ers consisted of POWs settled within the Empire in exchange for military service, most were simply indi vidual foreigners taken on as required, some being maintained on a permanent basis while others were employed only temporarily. Though it seems likely that provincial governors and field commanders sometimes hired their own, in every known instance they were hired directly by the central government, which called them *misthophoroi*, after their pay (*misthos* or *roga*). Consequently most were found in, or attached to, the central army. Pay was in theory distributed every two to six months but rarely materialised on time, despite the fact that delays often prompted mass desertions.

In the period from 1302 until the 1370s some mercenaries were hired in ready-organised companies (called *syntrophiai*) paid by their own leaders. The most famous was the Catalan 'Grand Company' of Roger de Flor, the Byzantine experience of which was probably the reason why subsequent mercenary companies only occasionally exceeded 100 men. Bitter memories of mass desertions in the 11th century, most significantly at Manzikert, had similarly taught the Byzantines that it was best if all mercenary units were kept to manageable proportions, and it was only when this lesson was forgotten after the 12th century that large-scale desertions resumed.

The following 'dictionary' of 12th–15th century foreign contingents should help the reader appreciate the truly cosmopolitan nature of late Byzantine armies.

Alans

Often referred to as *Massagetoi*, these were nominally-Christian Turks from the Caucasus, and in Byzantine service provided light, bow-armed cavalry. They are known to have been employed from the late 11th century to at least the mid 12th, and again in the mid 13th century and at the beginning of the 14th. The chronicler Muntaner says they were considered 'the best cavalry there is in the East' when about 5–8,000 were settled as military colonists in Thrace in 1301, receiving twice the pay of the best native troops. However, this contingent did not answer well to discipline, nor did they get on with the Catalans with whom they were brigaded in 1303–4, and altercations with the latter led to their utter destruction by the Catalans in 1306.

Albanians

These began to be found in Byzantine employ during the first half of the 14th century, but were utilised chiefly, if not exclusively, in Thessaly and the Morea, appearing in the latter in 1349. In the 1390s Theodore I Palaeologos (Despot 1383–1407) allowed about 10,000 Albanians to settle in the Morea in exchange for military service, and their numbers are unreliably claimed to have reached 30,000 by the 15th century. Serving principally as cavalry, they were the mainstay of the forces with which the Despots reconquered much of the Morea in the 1430s and 1440s. They invariably served under their own leaders, and apparently specialised as frontier guards.

Armenians

In the 12th–13th centuries contingents of Armenian auxiliaries raised in Cilicia were occasionally recorded fighting alongside Byzantine field armies in Northern Syria and Anatolia. The army of Theodore I of Nicaea, for instance, included Armenian troops

Byzantine warships were invariably lateen-rigged galleys, recorded in 1350 as having 100 to 300 oarsmen operating one or two banks of oars. Although some were probably still fitted with Greek fire siphons as late as the 1170s their armament afterwards is unknown, though there is little reason to suppose that – unlike Genoese and Venetian vessels – any ever carried gunpowder artillery even as late as 1453. The clean-shaven oarsmen of the 14th century galley depicted here, wearing characteristic European bonnets, are presumably Gazmouloi. (Instituto Ellenico di Venezia)

in 1214. Twelfth-century Cilician contingents were effectively indistinguishable from native Byzantine troops, but by the 13th century their equipment was becoming distinctly Westernised under the influence of the neighbouring Crusader principalities.

Bulgarians

After Michael VIII fielded an unspecified number of Bulgarians at the Battle of Pelagonia (1259) they appeared with increasing regularity until the second half of the 14th century. Apparently they were often hired as ready-formed companies of brigands, such as the 300-strong units led by Choiroboskos in 1303-4 and Sebastopoulos in 1329, and the 1,000 men raised by the former in 1305. These appear to have consisted exclusively of bow-armed light cavalry. Allied contingents were also occasionally supplied by Bulgaria's tsars during 1321–52, such as the 1,000 provided to Empress Anna in 1346.

Burgundians

The Duke of Burgundy sent 300 men to the assistance of Despot Constantine in the Morea in 1445, and stray Burgundians found their way into Byzantine service on other occasions in the 15th century.

Catalans

Occasionally employed since the 1270s, the largest contingent of *Katelanoi* ever hired by the Byzantines was Roger de Flor's Catalan 'Grand Company', totalling perhaps 1,500 cavalry, 4,000 *Almughavares* (an Arabic term best translated as 'raiders' or 'skirmishers') and 1,000 other infantry when it was hired in 1302. Unfortunately the company's successes prompted de Flor to arrogance and, eventually, open hostility towards the emperor. Instructions to reduce the strength of his force to 3,000 were ignored, so in 1305 the Byzantines had de Flor assassinated and dispersed the company by force. Even so, in 1307 one element re-entered Byzantine service.

Following an unsuccessful Aragonese-Veneto-Byzantine naval engagement against the Genoese outside Constantinople in 1352, 3–500 Catalans stayed on in John VI's service, being organised into a bodyguard unit. By 1354 only 100 of these were left, but the unit itself may have survived into the 15th century.

Military saint from a mid to late 14th century Serbian church fresco. Both the quiver, with its lid open to reveal the arrows point-uppermost, and the composite bow with its horn nocks, are well portrayed.

Cretans

Crete was part of the Empire until seized by Venice during the Fourth Crusade, so it is unsurprising to find numerous Cretan refugees subsequently seeking asylum within the Empire. In the late 13th century an unknown number of Cretans were settled in Asia Minor in exchange for service as cavalrymen, Pachymeres recording Cretan refugees to have formed a sizeable element of Andronikos II's armies. Doukas describes Cretans amongst Constantinople's defenders in 1422 as 'the most faithful subjects of the Empire'. In 1452 Venice specifically granted permission for the Empire to recruit Cretan soldiers and sailors, a privilege denied to other powers.

Cumans

In Byzantine service these Asiatic nomads served exclusively as horse-archers, and consequently were usually brigaded alongside Uzes, Seljuks and other Turkish troops. First employed at the end of the 11th century, Cumans constituted one of the most important elements of Byzantine armies until the first half of the 14th century, those in the central army being collectively referred to as the *Skythikon* (a term originally used to describe the army's Patzinak troops). In 1241 John III settled perhaps as many as 10,000 as military colonists in Thrace and Anatolia, from where they were frequently mustered for campaigns in Europe, certainly up until 1292 and possibly later. They seem to have eventually become Hellenised, a Greek-speaking Cuman even becoming *megas domestikos* under Andronikos II. Cuman troops in Byzantine employ in the 1320s derived from an auxiliary contingent loaned by Stefan Urosh II of Serbia to Michael IX (co-emperor 1294–1320) and never returned.

Englishmen

The English were found in Byzantine employ by the 1080s. During the course of the 12th century they were absorbed into the Varangian Guard in increasing numbers, so that by *c.* 1180 it was described as being 'of British race', even though it also contained Scandinavians until 1204. It was probably all but entirely English by 1272, when Michael VIII specifically refers to it as comprising *Englinvarrangoi*. It seems likely that the English 'men-at-arms' recorded amongst Constantinople's defenders during 1394–1402 were Varangian Guards. Like their Scandinavian predecessors, English guardsmen consisted of axe-armed infantry. The very last reference to axe-bearing soldiers 'of British race' occurs in 1404.

Georgians

Georgian mercenaries are occasionally recorded in the 12th century, being present, for instance, amongst the Byzantines fighting in Italy in the 1150s, and auxiliary contingents were later loaned to the

Mid 14th century Serbian fresco depicting St Eustathius Placidas in a lamellar corselet, with his triangular shield suspended by a guige-strap. The depiction of the shield as curved, admittedly exaggerated here, is confirmed by other sources.

Empire by King George IV (1212–23). Invariably cavalry, they were apparently armed with a mixture of bows and lances.

Hungarians

Contingents of Hungarian auxiliaries occur spasmodically in the 12th–13th centuries, such as in the army raised by John II in 1137 and that which fought for Michael VIII at Pelagonia in 1259. Those contingents for which details survive invariably consist entirely of cavalry.

'Latins'

Though some were Italians, Germans and Spaniards, Frenchmen constituted the majority of the Western mercenaries referred to in Byzantine sources as 'Latins', 'Franks' or 'Kelts'. They had been hired in considerable numbers since the 11th century, initially from Norman Italy and Sicily but subsequently chiefly from the Palestinian Crusader states until their demise, and thereafter via Frankish Greece. Their numbers increased considerably under the Latinophile Emperor Manuel I, so that after the Turks they were the predominant mercenary element. Though some were infantrymen, specifically specialists such as crossbowmen and, in the 15th century, handgunners, most were inevitably armoured cavalrymen.

Latin and, to a lesser extent, Cuman mercenaries

comprised the backbone of the Nicaean central army. The Nicaeans employed such large numbers of Latins, particularly under John III, that the rank of *megas konostablos* was created for the officer responsible for them (only occasionally himself a Latin). Their numbers waned from the 1260s, in step with a parallel increase in the use of Turkish and Cuman mercenaries, but revived during the civil wars of 1321–57. In the 13th century Latin troops in the central army were collectively referred to as the *Latinikon* or *Italikon* corps.

Not all Latins in Byzantine service were mercenaries. Contingents of allied auxiliaries also occasionally occurred, such as the Italians and Germans supplied to the Epirotes by Emperor Frederick II in 1230 and the 400 German knights provided in 1259 by his son Manfred, King of Sicily. The most celebrated auxiliary contingent was that of Marshal Boucicault in 1399, consisting of 600 men-at-arms, 600 varlets and 1,000 archers, all paid for by King Charles V of France. Most of these returned home the same year, but a sixth of their number remained in Constantinople until 1402.

Mongols

A 15th century Ottoman historian records Mongol auxiliaries in a Nicaean Byzantine army defeated by the Seljuks as early as the reign of Sultan Kai Kobad (1220–37). Though this is unrecorded elsewhere, Michael VIII had certainly concluded a treaty with the Ilkhan Hulagu by 1261 and in 1282 was provided with 4,000 Mongols by Nogai Khan of the Golden Horde, with which he marched against Thessaly. In 1305 Ilkhan Oljeitu promised 40,000 troops to

Serbian (left) and Bulgarian (right) armoured cavalrymen fighting as horse-archers, from mid 14th century manuscripts. There is no similar pictorial evidence of Byzantine cavalrymen using bows, though the fact that Byzantine archers were frequently brigaded alongside Cumans and Turks on the battlefield and must therefore have been mounted indicates that they did; and the English chronicler Ambroise actually records Isaac Komnenos of Cyprus firing two arrows at King Richard from horseback in 1191. Certainly composite bows are depicted amongst the weapons of most military saints in late Byzantine art. It can therefore be concluded that, despite having fallen out of favour from c. 1150 to c. 1350 – during which period Byzantine sources invariably describe their cavalrymen fighting only with lance and sword – the bow clearly never entirely disappeared.

Byzantine soldiers, 12th-13th centuries
1: Cavalryman
2: Man-at-arms
3: Infantryman

A

1: Almughavar mercenary, c. 1304
2: Cuman mercenary, c. 1300
3: Alan mercenary, 13th century

B

1: Byzantine soldier, c. 1295
2: Epirote Byzantine soldier, 14th century
3: Byzantine or Bulgarian infantryman, c. 1350

C

Byzantine soldiers,
14th century
1: Cavalryman
2: Infantryman
3: Archer, c. 1326

D

1: Serbian auxiliary, 14th century
2: Bulgarian auxiliary, c. 1345
3: Serbian knight, 15th century

E

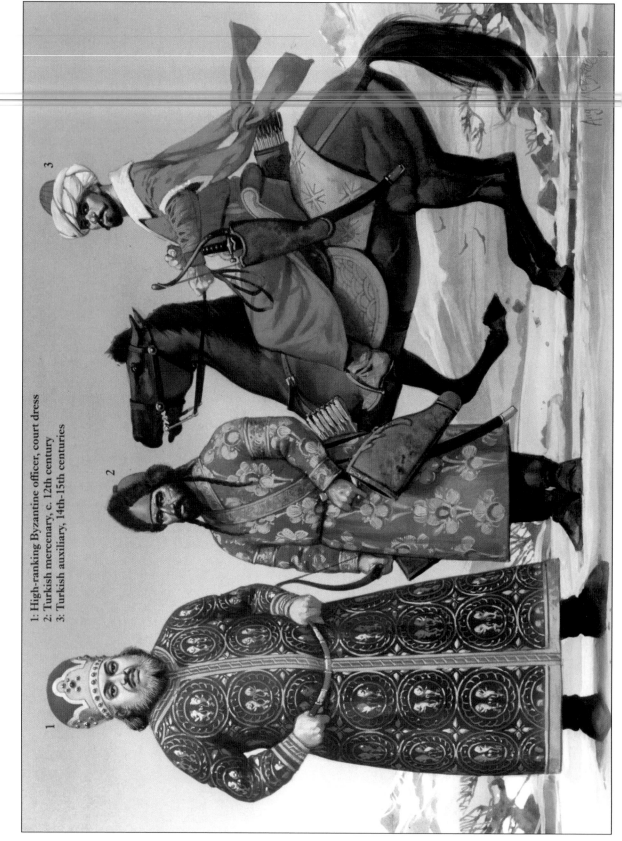

1: High-ranking Byzantine officer, court dress
2: Turkish mercenary, c. 12th century
3: Turkish auxiliary, 14th–15th centuries

F

1: Cuman mercenary,
   14th century
2: Albanian mercenary,
   15th century
3: Italian mercenary, 1453

1: Byzantine militia, 15th century
2: Byzantine cavalryman, 1438
3: Trapezuntine, 1461

H

Andronikos II, and in 1308 despatched 30,000 into Bithynia to recover numerous Byzantine towns from the Turks. The Mongols Andronikos subsequently fielded against the Serbs were perhaps an element of these.

Patzinaks

The Turkic Pechenegs or Patzinaks, often archaically referred to as 'Scyths', constituted the majority of the Empire's Asiatic mercenaries during the middle Byzantine period, but their employment was in decline by the 12th century. Patzinaks captured at Eski Zagra in 1122 were settled as military colonists in Thrace and Macedonia, and thrived there until the Latin Conquest in 1204, but the last record of Patzinak mercenaries in the field seems to date to 1136–39.

Russians

Auxiliaries were provided by various Russian princes in the 12th century. They probably served in the Varangian Guard.

Scandinavians

At the beginning of this period the Varangian Guard still consisted predominantly of Norwegians and Danes, and 'King Sverrir's Saga' claims that as late as 1195 Alexius III made a direct request to the kings of Scandinavia for 1,200 men to fill its ranks. 'Danish' guardsmen are last recorded in 1204.

Serbs

In the first half of the 12th century the Serbs were obliged to provide the Empire with 300 cavalry for campaigns in Asia Minor, a figure increased, following Serbia's defeat by Manuel I in 1150, to 500 for Asiatic campaigns and 2,000 for service in Europe. Others were provided by Serbian prisoners settled in Anatolia by John II in the 1120s. Even after Serbia's secession from the Empire, contingents of Serbian

An early 14th century portrayal of St Demetrius, patron saint of Thessalonika, killing Tsar Kalojan of Bulgaria (1197–1207). Kalojan's armour closely resembles that described by Theodore Palaeologos in 1326 as typical harness of the Westernised Byzantine soldiers to be found in Greece, comprising pourpoint, mail corselet, gorgeré (hood or collar?), cuirie, gambeson, 'greaves' (probably mail chausses), cuisses, and helmet. Kalojan's quilted cuisses have plate knee-guards attached.

Although from a 14th century Serbian mural, these military saints could as easily be Byzantines. They wear lamellar corselets and are armed with lance, sword and composite bow. The main figure has his helmet suspended by its chin-strap.

mercenaries and auxiliaries continued to be regularly encountered in Byzantine service. For instance, there were 600, or perhaps 1,000, in Michael VIII's army at Pelagonia. Allied contingents of Serbian auxiliaries (though not always actually composed of Serbs) steadily increased in size and importance during the first half of the 14th century. Stefan Urosh II, for instance, loaned Michael IX 2,000 Cuman cavalry in 1312, while John VI was provided with German mercenaries in 1342–43. The last instance of Serbs fighting for the Byzantines dates to 1352, when John V was provided with 4,000 cavalry.

Turks

Hired extensively during the middle Byzantine era, the employment of large numbers of Turks was revived under Michael VIII in the second half of the 13th century. He is recorded as having 5,000 Seljuks in his pay by 1262 when those associated with the central army were referred to as the *Persikon* corps.

From the 14th century on, when they constituted the largest foreign element of virtually every Byzantine field army, such contingents were normally of allied auxiliaries rather than mercenaries, receiving no pay but retaining whatever booty and prisoners fell into their hands. Umur of Aydin provided 2,000 such auxiliary cavalry for Andronikos III's Albanian campaign of 1337, subsequently supplying John VI Kantakouzenos with 6,000 in 1343 and perhaps 5,000 more in 1345, while the Amir of Saruhan provided the Empress Anna with 6,000 in 1346. Thereafter, however, such contingents usually consisted of Ottomans. John VI had 6,000 Ottoman auxiliary cavalry in 1345, 10,000 in 1348, and as many as 20,000 – responsible for the recapture of Thessalonika from the Serbs – by 1349. However, Kantakouzenos himself observed of such sizeable contingents that they were 'too numerous for the Romans to control', and tended to strike out on their own 'whenever there was hope of gain', as they did in 1354 when the 10–20,000 then nominally under his orders seized the city of Gallipoli for themselves. Yet despite this the services of Ottoman contingents were regularly sought by one side or the other in the Empire's numerous internal power struggles throughout the 14th and early 15th centuries.

Often to be found brigaded alongside the Turks in the 12th-14th centuries, and sometimes indistinguishable from them, was a corps of regular troops called the *Tourkopouloi* or 'sons of Turks'. Nominally consisting of the descendants of Christianised Turks or the issue of mixed unions, on occasion they included natives of the Empire's Anatolian provinces, who Pachymeres records shaving their heads Turkish-fashion in order to join them. They are rarely encountered following the desertion of 1,000 during the Battle of Apros in 1305, though some of the deserters rejoined in 1312.

Uzes

A Turkish people very similar in appearance and identical in armament to the Cumans and/or Seljuks (from whom some sources have difficulty distinguishing them), the Uzes were found in the Balkans in the 11th–12th centuries. The Byzantines employed them in considerable numbers, and they apparently constituted the largest part of the Empire's Turkish mercenaries at the time of both Manzikert

Soldier from a fresco in the Church of the Brontochion, Mistra, executed shortly after 1449 and thought to depict Constantine XI. The accuracy of the very traditional equipment portrayed is impossible to determine since we know virtually nothing about 15th century Byzantine armour. Note he carries a small circular shield; though uncommon, these never entirely disappeared amongst Byzantine cavalrymen.

(1071) and Myriokephalon (1176), but disappear after the latter date.

Vlachs

First employed in the 11th century, Vlach or Wallachian troops were regularly utilised throughout this period, despite being considered 'faithless and perverse'. There were Wallachian mercenaries in the

Epirote army at Pelagonia and in Michael IX's armies at the beginning of the 14th century, while the *voivode* of Dobrudja sent 1,000 auxiliaries to support Empress Anna in 1346. Wallachian mercenaries also assisted in the defence of Constantinople in 1422, and the future *voivode* Vlad II Dracul was 'an officer in the army' of John VIII.

THE END OF THE EMPIRE

The civil wars of the 14th century had exhausted the last of the Empire's diminishing resources. Repeated Byzantine appeals to the West thereafter for military and financial aid, even when made in person by Manuel II in 1399–1403 and John VIII in 1437–39, generally fell on ears deafened by religious discord (the Empire being Orthodox while Europe was Catholic), and even when this difficulty was nominally overcome by the unpopular Union of the churches in 1439 the situation remained effectively unchanged. Under continuous Ottoman pressure the Empire's frontiers continued to contract. Bertrandon de la Brocquière, visiting Constantinople in 143. observed that by then Byzantine territory extende no more than two days' ride from the city walls.

By the time the Ottomans appeared before Con stantinople's walls for the final time in 1453, wha passed for the Imperial army probably comprise between about 1,000 and 1,500 men. By what mus have been a supreme effort, however, a garrison o some 7–9,000 fighting men was assembled, of whom according to George Sphrantzes – ordered to take census of them by Emperor Constantine XI – 4,77 were Byzantines. The balance of 2–4,000 mer (Leonard of Chios says 'hardly as many as 3,000') along with some two to three dozen ships, several o which were equipped with guns, were provided b foreign volunteers and mercenaries, mainl Venetians, Genoese and Catalans looking after thei commercial interests. Many of the Genoese actuall came from the republic's colony of Galata, just acros the Golden Horn from Constantinople, despite thi suburb remaining technically neutral in the conflict.

Most prominent of the Genoese commander was Giovanni Giustiniani Longo, who received the rank of *protostrator* and was overall commander of the city's defences. He had arrived with two galleys and 3–400 men (6–700 if one counts the galley crews equipped and raised entirely at his own expense. Th

Obverse and reverse of a medallion by Pisanello (1439) portraying Emperor John VIII. His dress and equipment betray unmistakable Turkish influence. (British Museum)

men, described as 'in full armour', were armed with crossbows, handguns and even cannon. Venice's contribution to the defence, under the command of their *bailli* in Constantinople, Girolamo Minotto, comprised five ships, which landed a total of 1,000 men. Another largely Italian contingent had arrived with the papal legate, Cardinal Isidore, in 1452, consisting of 200 handgunners and crossbowmen. At least 50 of these were Neapolitans, but the rest were hired on Chios (as, coincidentally, were some of Giustiniani's men).

The Ottoman siege began on 2 April 1453. Figures of up to 400 ships and 700,000 men are recorded for Mehmed II's forces, but the figures given by a Venetian eye-witness, Nicolò Barbaro, of 82–92 warships plus transports, and 160,000 men (tallying with Doukas' reference to the Ottomans outnumbering the defenders by 20 to one), seem more probable. In addition the Sultan had brought together a massive artillery train that included both guns and conventional siege-engines. A Genoese eye-witness states that there were 200 'guns and tormentia' in all, and Barbaro that there were 12 principal guns, which various sources record firing shot of between 90 and as much as 850 kg. (200–1,900 lbs). The largest of these was so massive that it could barely be moved by 150 yoke of oxen.

The Ottoman artillery bombardment began on 6 April, with their guns firing 100–120 times a day thereafter until the end of the siege. The defenders

Drawing by Pisanello of Byzantine horse-harness, 1438. By as early as the 13th century horses were generally in short supply, and most Byzantine soldiers provided their own. Heavy cavalrymen rode destriers like their Western counterparts, lighter-armed horsemen riding mares or geldings. Arabian, Damascene and Edessan horses were considered the best in the 12th century, but would have been largely unobtainable by the 14th, when Hungarian, Thessalian and, later, Turkish mounts seem to have predominated. (Louvre, Copyright Réunion des Musées Nationaux)

were eventually obliged to fall back behind the outer wall as considerable portions were reduced to rubble, further damage being caused by the recoil of their own guns and by mining and counter-mining operations which criss-crossed back and forth beneath the foundations.

On 18 May a premature attempt by the Turks to bring up a siege-tower in preparation for a general assault ended ignominiously when it was set aflame as soon as it came within range of the defenders. Not long afterwards parts of the inner wall finally collapsed in the vicinity of the Gate of St. Romanus, and under cover of darkness the Turks set about bridging the huge moat with piles of rubble in preparation for the final assault, which began in the small hours of 29 May. The first two waves of the assault force, consisting respectively of irregulars (many of them Christian conscripts from Greece, Hungary and the Balkans) and Anatolian troops, were beaten back from the breaches, many being consumed by Greek fire hurled from the walls. However, the third Ottoman line, made up of Janissaries and other elite troops, pressed home its attack, at the height of which, just before dawn, Giustiniani was desperately wounded. His withdrawal from the scene of the fighting, followed soon after by the majority of his leaderless men, so demoralised the defenders that the Turks were subsequently able to break through in several places.

Despite counter-attacks launched in the street by various Byzantine and Italian commanders, including the emperor himself, this marked the end of organised resistance. All those that could now fled for the handful of ships anchored along the Golden Horn. Giustiniani was amongst those who escaped, getting as far as Chios before he succumbed to his wounds. Constantine XI, however, died anonymously in the streets, sword in hand, just one of 4,000 Byzantines and Italians killed that day.

THE EMPIRE OF TREBIZOND

Trebizond had become effectively independent of Constantinople shortly before the latter fell to the forces of the Fourth Crusade in 1204. With the assistance of troops provided by their aunt, Queen Thamar of Georgia, this tiny 'Empire' on the south-

Fifteenth-century Turkish cavalry, from Breydenbach's Peregrinationes. *Though some wear turbans others wear characteristically Balkan headwear; these are probably the hats 'like those worn at rustic merry-makings' recorded by Pero Tafur in 1437.*

Rumeli Hisar ('European Fortress'), which Sultan Mehmed II built on the European shore of the Bosporus in just four months in 1452. Intended to command the straits in preparation for the siege of Constantinople, it was initially named Boghaz-kesen ('Cutter of the Channel').

eastern coastline of the Black Sea was founded by two brothers, Alexius and David (the latter subsequently, but briefly, independent ruler of Paphlagonia), who were grandsons of Emperor Andronikos I Komnenos (1183–85), from whom the Trapezuntine Emperor was known as the *Megas Komnenos*. Its survival thereafter depended more on diplomacy and the country's rugged Pontic geography than military might, particularly after the Seljuks overran its western half in 1214 (in the process separating its frontier from the Empire of Nicaea). This rendered the 'Empire' an inconsequential petty state of diminutive proportions. Towards the close of Andronikos Gidon's reign (1222–35) Seljuk suzerainty was acknowledged, and his successors were thereafter obliged to supply 200 men to the Seljuk army when called for (compared to 400 supplied by the Emperor of Nicaea). Following the Mongol defeat of the Seljuks at Kuzadagh in 1243 suzerainty was transferred to the Great Khan and subsequently, in all probability, to the Ilkhanids and, later still, to Tamerlane (who called for the Trapezuntines to provide him with 20 galleys for use against the Ottoman Turks in 1402, though there is no evidence that they obliged).

Trebizond's military strength, never considerable, was crippled in 1330–55 by a series of civil wars between the powerful provincial nobility and the Imperial party. Despite over-optimistic expectations by foreigners in the 15th century that it could raise 15–25,000 men, the largest recorded Trapezuntine field army, assembled in 1366 to impress the Amir of the neighbouring Aq Qoyunlu (White Sheep Turks), actually totalled only about 2,000 men. Other evidence confirms that Trebizond's armies were invariably small, including a Moslem account of *c.* 1350 that describes its soldiers as 'few in number and ill-equipped'. In 1355, for instance, the loss of at most 400 men in a battle against the Turks was considered a major disaster, while in 1380 half of an army that had been divided into two parts comprised just 600 infantrymen (the other half consisting of cavalry and 'another very large party of foot-soldiers'). Small wonder, therefore, that after the mid 14th century Trebizond largely abandoned military confrontation in favour of diplomatic marriage alliances with its powerful Turkish neighbours, in particular maintaining close relations with the Aq Qoyunlu by this means for several generations.

The Empire's frontier defence was in the hands of local warlords of mixed Byzantine and native (chiefly Laz or *Tzannoi*) descent, who maintained their own fortresses and garrisons in exchange for official recognition of their lands as *pronoiai*. They were justifiably considered little better than bandits by travellers, from whom exorbitant sums were extorted in exchange for escorts and safe passage. Most of the Empire was similarly responsible for its own defence, being organised into several territorial units in which the owners of smallholdings were known by traditional Byzantine military terms such as *strategoi, stratiotai* and *kastrophylakes*, and were obliged to perform military service when called upon.

A very small central army also seems to have existed. This is probably represented by the troop of 100 cavalrymen which in 1370 accompanied Emperor Alexius III (1349–90) on campaign, and the 140 men assigned by Manuel III (1390–1417) to escort the Spanish ambassador Ruy Gonzalez de Clavijo in 1404. Such household troops probably consisted of mercenaries, to whom there are occasional references throughout this period. Some such mercenaries were Georgians, but most were Turks, so that the larger part were, unsurprisingly, cavalry. A few Latins may also have found their way even this far east; certainly David of Paphlagonia is credited with having 300 Latins in his employ *c*. 1207. Probably these were Italians, since both Venice and, more especially, Genoa maintained colonies in Trebizond.

Allied contingents were also sometimes made available, or at least promised, by the Empire's Turkish and Georgian neighbours. Many of these were allied by marriage to the Imperial family. In April 1404, for instance, two of the four principal allies of Manuel III resulted from such matrimonial ties (his nephew Altamur of Limnia and brother-in-law Suleiman of Chalybia). Similarly, when John IV (1429–58) planned a coalition against the Ottomans in 1457 its most important members were his brother-in-law the King of Georgia, and the Aq Qoyunlu Amir Uzun Hassan, who, by two different marriage alliances, was simultaneously his nephew and son-in-law.

It was not until 1442 that the Ottomans launched their first assault on Trebizond. Though the city

Though the land walls have largely lain in ruins since 1453, portions of Constantinople's massive fortifications remain impressive even today. These two views are of the sympathetically restored fortress of the Golden Gate.

Right: Section through Constantinople's land walls. (Cambridge University Press)

walls withstood both this siege and another in 1456, the Empire was obliged to make substantial tribute payments following the second attack. It was a request by John IV's brother and successor David (1458–61) that this tribute be remitted which prompted the third and final attack in 1461, when a massive Ottoman force of allegedly 60,000 horse, 80,000 foot and 1-300 ships descended on the city. The coalition which John IV and David had so painstakingly put together instantly fell apart, isolating Trebizond, which surrendered in August after a siege lasting just a few weeks. The *Megas Komnenos* David, initially sent into exile, was executed two years later.

Recommended reading

M. Angold *A Byzantine Government in Exile: Government and Society under the Laskarids of Nicaea 1204–1261* (1975); J.W. Barker *Manuel II Palaeologus 1391–1425* (1969); M.C. Bartusis *The Late Byzantine Army: Arms and Society 1204–1453* (1992); S. Blöndal *The Varangians of Byzantium* (1978); C.W. Brand *Byzantium Confronts the West 1180–1204* (1968) and (trans.) *Deeds of John and Manuel Comnenus* (1976); R. Dawkins 'The Later History of the Varangian Guard' *Journal of Roman Studies* XXXVII (1947); G.T. Dennis *Byzantium and the Franks 1350–1420* (1982); D.J. Geanakoplos *The Emperor Michael Palaeologus and the West 1258–1282* (1959); Lady Goodenough (trans.) *The Chronicle of Muntaner* (1967); H.W. Hazard (Ed.) *A History of the Crusades* Vols. II–III (1969–75); J.R. Melville Jones (trans.) *Nicolò Barbaro: Diary of the Siege of Constantinople 1453* (1969) and *The Siege of Constantinople 1453: Seven Contemporary Accounts* (1972); A.E. Laiou *Constantinople and the Latins: The Foreign Policy of Andronicus II 1282–1328* (1972); A. Lowe *The Catalan Vengeance* (1972); H.E. Lurier (trans.) *Crusaders as Chroniclers: The Chronicle of the Morea* (1964); E.H. McNeal (trans.) *The Conquest of Constantinople: Robert de Clari* (1936); P. Magdalino *The Empire of Manuel I Komnenos 1143–1180* (1993); H.J. Magoulias (trans.) *Decline and Fall of Byzantium to the Ottoman Turks, by Doukas* (1975) and *O City of Byzantium: Annals of Niketas Choniates* (1984); F. Marzials (trans.) *Villehardouin's Chronicle of the Fourth Crusade and the Conquest of Constantinople* (1908); W. Miller *Trebizond: The Last Greek Empire* (1926); D.M. Nicol *The Last Centuries of Byzantium 1261–1453* (1972) and *The Despotate of Epiros 1267–*

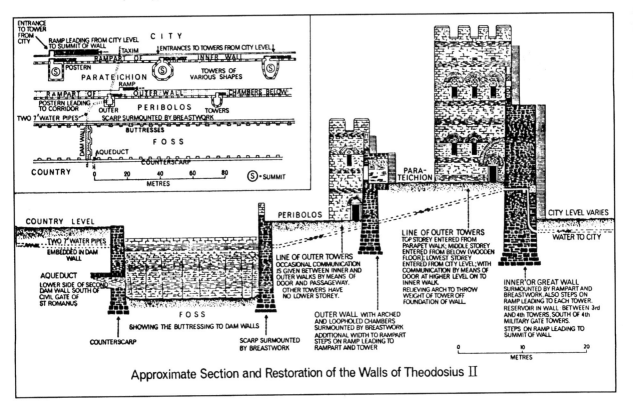

Approximate Section and Restoration of the Walls of Theodosius II

1479 (1984); M. Philippides (trans.) *The Fall of the Byzantine Empire: A Chronicle by George Sphrantzes 1401–1477* (1980); D.E. Queller *The Fourth Crusade: The Conquest of Constantinople 1201–1204* (1978); C.T. Riggs (trans.) *History of Mehmed the Conqueror by Kritovoulos* (1954); S. Runciman *The Fall of Constantinople 1453* (1965) and *Mistra: Byzantine Capital of the Peloponnese* (1980); G.C. Soulis *The Serbs and Byzantium during the Reign of Tsar Stephen Dusan and his Successors* (1984).

THE PLATES

A: Byzantine soldiers, 12th–13th centuries

Although foreign influences – especially Italo-Norman and Turkish – were considerable by the 12th century, Byzantine equipment portrayed in contemporary pictures retains several distinctive characteristics, most notably the leather fringes and *pteruges* at waist and shoulders. Though lamellar and scale armour remained in use until at least the 14th century, mail armour predominated. Corselets came in various styles, usually with short sleeves but sometimes long-sleeved or sleeveless. Lighter-armed men generally wore a hip-length leather corselet instead, this invariably having a horizontal breast-band, the purpose of which may have been to secure the two halves of the cuirass in place (though this does not explain why such breast-bands also occur in conjunction with mail corselets).

Characteristic armament of 12th century Byzantine cavalrymen consisted of lance and sword. Though both wooden and cane lances were used the adoption of the Western custom of couching the lance underarm – which had become normal Byzantine practice by the 1150s – meant that the former were preferred. The chronicler Choniates observed that 'flexible reed spears were not at all adequate' for this sort of fighting. Byzantine swords were indistinguishable from those of Western Europe (in 1400 Emperor Manuel II even expressed the view that English swords were copied from those of Byzantium). Kinnamos, writing early in the 13th century, states that maces were also customarily carried by Byzantine cavalrymen.

Shields were principally made of light, soft wood, edged in leather or iron, covered with parchment or leather and usually painted, mostly with abstract or geomorphic devices in the 12th century (these apparently giving way to geometric patterns – principally of chevrons, stripes and blocks of colour – in the 13th–14th centuries). Until the late 13th century most were of the almond-shaped variety of A1, but some infantrymen continued to use circular shields of various sizes.

A1 is based on 12th–13th century Cappadocian frescoes from the Göreme area, in particular that of 1282–1304 at Kirk Dam, while A2 is from mid 13th century manuscripts illuminated in Acre, often in Byzantine style and sometimes copied from Byzantine originals. His appearance is similar to that of contemporary Western European men-at-arms. Other manuscripts illuminated at Acre depict Byzantine troops who, in heaumes and surcoats, are indistinguishable from Western knights. Significantly the

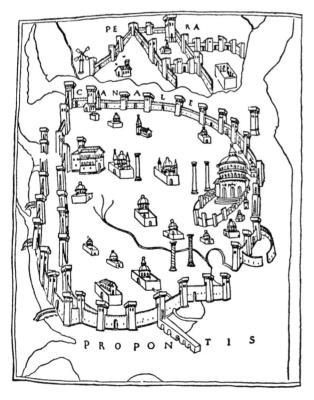

A simplistic map of Constantinople drawn in 1422 by a Florentine traveller, Buondelmonte. The massive church of Hagia Sophia stands on the right, while the large building towards the top left is the Blachernae Palace. Note that the double land walls extend north from the Golden Gate fortress only as far as the Blachernae district. Beyond the Golden Horn lies the suburb of Pera, or Galata.

Empire is known to have been importing arms and armour from the West, via Italy, by 1261 at the very latest.

A3 is a typical Anatolian Byzantine infantryman, based largely on Queen Melissande's Psalter of *c.* 1131–43. Infantry spears were generally about 2.4 metres (8 ft) long throughout the late Byzantine period. Other light-armed infantry carried only a bow and shield, while occasionally slingers are recorded (as amongst the Epirotes attacking Prilep in 1257).

B1: Almughavar mercenary, 1304

Characteristic weapons of the *Amogavaroi* were a 'coutell' (a spear long enough that it needed to be broken short for close combat) and between two and four javelins (*azagaya*), thrown with such 'speed and violence' that they could kill an armoured man. So effective was this weapon combination in an Almughavar's experienced hands that on one occasion a single warrior brought down five armoured horsemen, killing two with javelins and bringing down the horses of two more (one with a javelin, the other with his spear), while disabling the fifth with a thrown stone.

B2: Cuman mercenary, c. 1300

The sequence of Hungarian church murals at Vel'kej Lomnici on which this figure is based show that under the quilted hood he wears his hair very long, which was normal practice amongst the Cumans (see plate G1). The fact that he wears spurs indicates western influence, the Cumans more usually controlling their horses with just their heels and a short whip. Typically armed with a composite bow and sabre, other weapons might include a mace, light spear and javelins. Small shields, mostly circular but under Byzantine or Serbian influence sometimes almond-shaped, were also used. Superlative horsemen, Cumans are recorded to have been accompanied on campaign by up to 10–12 remounts, these being ridden in rotation so that a fresh mount was always available.

B3: Alan mercenary, 13th century

Alani in Byzantine employ invariably served as light cavalry. The majority were armed with a composite bow and a sabre, a smaller number probably adding a light lance and, sometimes, a smallish, circular shield. Even in Byzantine service they were accompanied by their families on campaign, these travelling

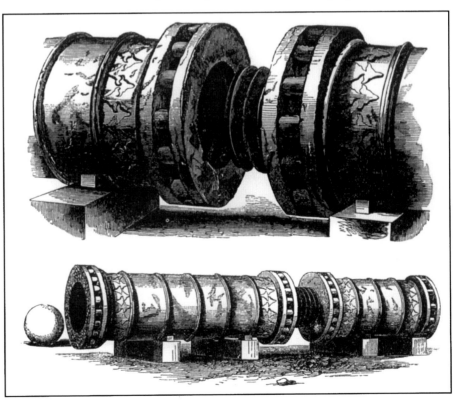

An Ottoman hooped iron gun of 1464, identical to pieces used against Constantinople. Kritoboulos records that the very largest of Mehmed II's guns in 1453 was 8.17 metres (26.8ft) long, made in two halves that screwed together. The bore was 76cm (30in.) in the front half (for the shot) and 25cm (10in.) in the back half (for the charge). In the illustrated example the halves weighed 8–9 tons each.

in large wagons which were drawn up in a defensive laager around their camp-sites at night.

C1: Byzantine soldier, c. 1295

The type of armour worn by this soldier from Byzantine Macedonia (based largely on a church mural in Ohrid) flourished in Byzantium and neighbouring Serbia during the period *c.* 1280–1330, and perhaps until *c.* 1350. It typically comprised a mail-lined 'waistcoat' worn over a leather corselet and, under that, scale or lamellar body-armour and a separate, rigid collar of vertical laminae. Sabres and sabre-hilted swords began to make an appearance amongst Byzantines and Serbs alike at about this time.

C2: Epirote Byzantine soldier, 14th century

Although the almond-shaped shield of C1 could still be found in occasional use as late as *c.* 1350, by the late 13th century it was being displaced by the long, straight-sided triangular variety carried here. Mostly about 45cm (18in.) wide but varying in height between 90–150cm (3–5ft), these appear to have been of very light construction. The spurs worn by this figure (based on several Thessalonikan depictions of St Demetrius) indicate western influence.

C3: Byzantine or Bulgarian infantryman, c. 1350

Contemporary pictures show that the equipment of the average soldier was virtually identical on both sides of the Bulgaro-Byzantine frontier by the mid 14th century. This particular warrior, from a fresco of 1350–55 in the Monastery of Zemen, is typical. Most wore a short mail corselet with short sleeves and occasionally a collar, though some substituted lamellar armour. Shields varied somewhat in shape, the Bulgarians favouring the conventional Western European heater-shield over the longer, straight-sided triangular Byzantine variety (though they used both), and also still used bucklers.

D: Byzantine soldiers, 14th century

These soldiers are from pictures in the *Romance of Alexander the Great*. Men armoured as heavily as D1 would have been uncommon, armoured horses even more so (this whole manuscript contains only two armoured horses and one soldier with mail over his face). Doubtless such comprehensive armour would have been available only to soldiers of elite guard units, some of whom were still uniformed. Pseudo-Kodinos describes the Vardariots wearing red, and the *Tzakones* sky blue (embroidered on breast and back with two white lions face to face). Gregoras mentions uniforms in the mid 14th century, while the 16th century Ottoman historian Bitlisi mentions that Byzantine soldiers customarily wore scarlet.

The source shows soldiers equipped like D2 fighting both on foot and on horseback. Note that he still carries an almond-shaped shield, which gener-

The costumes of these Trapezuntine warriors, from a 15th century tomb in Trebizond's Hagia Sophia, clearly demonstrate the Turkish influence prevalent amongst the local Byzantine and Laz population. The mounted figures, below, wear white hats, yellow boots and red coats (one with a white pattern), while the standing figure, right, wears a white coat and yellow tunic.

ally disappeared at about this time. D3's quilted armour is identical to that found in Western European sources of the same date, the terms *pourpoint* and *gambeson* used to describe such corselets both occurring in a list of Byzantine arms dating to 1326. His arrow-quiver is of Persian type rather than the more usual Asiatic variety.

E1: Serbian auxiliary, 14th century

The frescoes of *c.* 1309–14 on which this figure is based demonstrate that 14th century Serbian equipment, like 14th century Bulgarian, differed little from that of Byzantium, though the Serbs, whilst making some use of the triangular shield by then preferred in the Empire, continued to favour the almond-shaped variety. Their preferred weapon combination appears to have been lance (still often wielded overarm), sword, mace and composite bow. The fact that Serbian armoured cavalry of the 13th and 14th centuries were prepared to fight as horse-archers is confirmed by Kantakouzenos' military

memoirs and pictures in Serbian manuscripts. Certainly the Serbs in the Nicaean army at the Battle of Pelagonia in 1259 were horse-archers.

E2: Bulgarian auxiliary, c. 1345

Pictorial sources demonstrate that the similarity between Bulgarian and Byzantine equipment persisted until Bulgaria fell to the Ottoman Turks at the end of the 14th century. Bulgarian costume, however, remained distinctly Balkan. The source for this figure is the *Manasses Codex* made for Tsar Ivan Alexander (1331–65), the illustrations of which indicate that the long gown often concealed light body-armour (Bulgarian mail or lamellar corselets often reaching only to the waist or hips). All Bulgarian cavalrymen were customarily armed with a composite bow, though their heavy cavalry at least also carried a lance.

E3: Serbian knight, 15th century

Under constant pressure from the Ottomans throughout the second half of the 14th century, Serbia began to import a growing volume of its arms from the West, in particular from Venice and Lombardy. By the 15th century better-equipped Serbs had become indistinguishable from their Italian counterparts, except in retaining a shield (probably in response to the Ottomans' dependence on archery). Ironically contingents of Serbian heavy cavalry consequently appeared in most Ottoman field armies during the first half of the 15th century, becoming famous for the effectiveness of their close-order charge. A 1,500-strong Serbian contingent even attended the siege of Constantinople in 1453.

F1: High-ranking Byzantine officer, court dress

Taken from a manuscript portrait of *c.* 1342, this is Alexius Apokaukos, *megas doux* 1340–45, a devious manipulator responsible for deliberately provoking the civil war of 1341–47 to further his own ambitions. Despite owing his initial advancement at court to John Kantakouzenos, he was nevertheless the principal supporter of John's adversary, the Empress Anna, until murdered by political prisoners while visiting a jail. The style of his long, ornate gown is typical of traditional 13th–15th century Byzantine upper-class dress, which was invariably bright and richly embroidered, often in gold thread.

F2: Turkish mercenary, 12th century

Uzes and Seljuks were both employed in large numbers until the 1170s, and we know from accounts of the Battle of Myriokephalon (1176) that they were, to all intents and purposes, indistinguishable. Predictably most were light horse-archers, but some were armoured (Kinnamos, for instance, records 'an armoured regiment of Turks' in the Byzantine army at Semlin in 1167). Those that settled in the Empire often took Byzantine wives and sometimes adopted Christianity, embracing Byzantine culture so thoroughly that it is not uncommon to find Turks holding senior posts in the Imperial hierarchy.

F3: Turkish auxiliary, 14th–15th centuries

Ottoman soldiers in Byzantine employ customarily consisted of light cavalry. These were generally armed with a composite bow, to which most added a sabre and some a light lance. A small, round wooden shield was also not uncommon. Their dress was heavily influenced by Balkan costume, consisting of baggy trousers, several long cotton robes worn one over another, and an outer robe of felt described as both light and waterproof. By the 15th century this usually had very long, slit sleeves which were customarily tied behind the back in action. In addition the long robes were often tucked into the top of the baggy trousers for freedom of movement. Damascene leather boots, and a turban (usually white) wrapped round a red cap, completed their costume.

G1: Cuman mercenary, 14th century

The costume of this warrior, from the famous *Képes Krónika* manuscript dating to the 1360s, is more typical than that of plate B2, and is similarly recorded in numerous 14th century sources. The characteristic wide-brimmed hats they all depict vary somewhat in shape, but invariably have the brim slit at the front or sides and turned up or down in different ways. Note his fair hair, which gave rise to the names *Polovtsy* and *Falven* by which the Cumans were known to the Russians and Germans, both deriving from words meaning 'yellow'.

G2: Albanian mercenary, 15th century

This figure, based largely on a 15th century portrait of the resistance leader Skanderbeg (1443–68), de-

picts characteristic Albanian costume, which consisted of a tall, broad-brimmed hat; sleeveless tunic; and a coat with extremely long sleeves, from which the arms usually emerged through a slit at the shoulder or elbow. It was from the Albanians that this fashion was copied by both Turks and Italians (the latter passing it on to Western Europe during the 15th century). The coat sometimes concealed a mail corselet, but most Albanians went unarmoured. Typical armament consisted of a light 3–3.7 metre (10–12ft) lance with a blade at each end (the *zagaie*), a straight, broad sword, and a heavy mace.

G3: Italian mercenary, 1453

Many of the Western mercenaries and volunteers who assisted in the final defence of Constantinople in 1453 were armed with handguns and crossbows, though spears and javelins are also recorded. The majority, being seamen, would have worn only light armour, or none at all, but a proportion – 3–400 of Giustiniani's men, for instance, and some of the Venetians – wore plate half-armour.

H1: Byzantine militiaman, 15th century

The men who constituted the greater part of the Byzantine defenders of Constantinople in 1453 were inexperienced civilians. These are described by Leonard of Chios as wielding their arms 'according to the light of nature rather than with any skill', and

we know from other sources that town-dwelling Byzantine civilians were largely ignorant of warfare and invariably reluctant to fight: the fact that several thousand rallied to Constantinople's defence in 1453 is actually exceptional. Leonard records them being armed mostly with swords, spears and shields, a smaller number having bows; however, the few that he mentions as being crossbow-armed were probably regular soldiers. From Doukas we know that others were armed with slings. Though Leonard also states that 'the majority' had helmets and leather or metal corselets (type not specified) this seems unlikely.

H2: Byzantine cavalryman, 1438

Pisanello's medal of John VIII, and his sketches of John's retinue in Italy, are the sources for this figure. The adoption of Turkish fashions had begun in Constantinople in the mid 14th century, and this man's appearance indicates that it was by now the dominant influence; even his shallow saddle and the slit nostrils of his horse conform to Turkish practice. There may be no evidence that 15th century Byzantine cavalrymen actually fought like the Turks, but it is significant that when Bertrandon de la Brocquière

The fall of Trebizond, from a painted Florentine cassone of c. 1462. The Byzantine defenders, armed with composite bows, curved sabres and spears, can only be distinguished from their Ottoman opponents by the substitution of tall, plumed hats for turbans.

visited Constantinople in 1433 he saw one of John's brothers and a score of horsemen practising horse-archery in the Hippodrome. He records that 'this exercise they had adopted from the Turks, and it was one of which they were endeavouring to make themselves masters'.

H3: Trapezuntine soldier, 1461

The extent of Turkish influence in the Empire of Trebizond is confirmed by Clavijo in 1404, who records that its soldiers 'make use of the sword and bow, the like of what arms the Turks employ, and they ride after the fashion of these last'. Costume was similarly oriental, with bright colours such as scarlet and green predominating. The hat worn here is probably one such as Clavijo saw being worn by the *Megas Komnenos*, which he describes as tall, trimmed with marten fur, with gold cords running up the sides and a plume of crane feathers.

INDEX

(References to illustrations are shown in **bold**. Plates are shown with page and caption locators in brackets.)